THE ILLUSTRATED POETS

THE ILLUSTRATED POETS

Love Poems

AURUM PRESS

First published 1995 by Aurum Press Ltd
25 Bedford Avenue, London WC1B 3AT

A catalogue record of this book is available from
the British Library

ISBN 1 85410 316 4

2 4 6 8 10 9 7 5 3
1997 1998 1999 1996

Picture research by Juliet Brightmore

Manufactured in China by Imago

CONTENTS

Love Poems

WILLIAM SHAKESPEARE
(1564–1616)

'Let me not to the marriage
of true minds'

Let me not to the marriage of true minds
Admit impediments; love is not love
Which alters when it alteration finds
Or bends with the remover to remove.
O, no, it is an ever-fixèd mark
That looks on tempests and is never shaken;
It is the star to every wand'ring bark,
Whose worth's unknown, although his
     height be taken.
Love's not Time's fool, though rosy lips and
     cheeks
Within his bending sickle's compass come;
Love alters not with his brief hours and
     weeks,
But bears it out even to the edge of doom.
    If this be error, and upon me proved,
    I never writ, nor no man ever loved.

JOHN DONNE
(1572–1631)

Elegy: To His Mistress Going to Bed

Come, Madam, come, all rest my powers defy,
Until I labour, I in labour lie.
The foe oft-times having the foe in sight,
Is tired with standing though they never fight.
Off with that girdle, like heaven's zone glistering,
But a far fairer world encompassing.
Unpin that spangled breastplate which you wear,
That th' eyes of busy fools may be stopped there.
Unlace yourself, for that harmonious chime
Tells me from you, that now 'tis your bed time.
Off with that happy busk, which I envy,
That still can be, and still can stand so nigh.
Your gown going off, such beauteous state reveals,
As when from flowery meads th' hill's shadow steals.
Off with that wiry coronet and show
The hairy diadem which on you doth grow;
Now off with those shoes, and then safely tread
In this love's hallowed temple, this soft bed.
In such white robes heaven's angels used to be
Received by men; thou angel bring'st with thee
A heaven like Mahomet's paradise; and though
Ill spirits walk in white, we easily know
By this these angels from an evil sprite,
Those set our hairs, but these our flesh upright.

Licence my roving hands, and let them go
Before, behind, between, above, below.
O my America, my new found land,
My kingdom, safeliest when with one man manned,
My mine of precious stones, my empery,
How blessed am I in this discovering thee!
To enter in these bonds, is to be free;
Then where my hand is set, my seal shall be.
    Full nakedness, all joys are due to thee.
As souls unbodied, bodies unclothed must be,
To taste whole joys. Gems which you women use
Are like Atlanta's balls, cast in men's views,
That when a fool's eye lighteth on a gem,
His earthly soul may covet theirs, not them.
Like pictures, or like books' gay coverings made
For laymen, are all women thus arrayed;
Themselves are mystic books, which only we
Whom their imputed grace will dignify
Must see revealed. Then since I may know,
As liberally, as to a midwife, show
Thyself: cast all, yea, this white linen hence,
Here is no penance, much less innocence.
    To teach thee, I am naked first, why then
What needst thou have more covering than a
        man.

WILLIAM BLAKE
(1757–1827)

The Clod & the Pebble
from
SONGS OF EXPERIENCE

'Love seeketh not Itself to please,
'Nor for itself hath any care;
'But for another gives its ease,
'And builds a Heaven in Hell's despair.'

So sang a little Clod of Clay,
Trodden with the cattle's feet:
But a Pebble of the brook
Warbled out these metres meet:

'Love seeketh only Self to please,
'To bind another to its delight;
'Joys in another's loss of ease,
'And builds a Hell in Heaven's despite.'

ROBERT BURNS
(1759–96)

'A red, red rose'

O my Luve's like a red, red rose,
 That's newly sprung in June;
O my Luve's like the melodie
 That's sweetly play'd in tune. –

As fair art thou, my bonnie lass,
 So deep in luve am I;
And I will love thee still, my Dear,
 Till a' the seas gang dry. –

Till a' the seas gang dry, my Dear,
 And the rocks melt wi' the sun:
I will love thee still, my Dear,
 While the sands o' life shall run. –

And fare thee weel, my only Luve!
 And fare thee weel, a while!
And I will come again, my Luve,
 Tho' it were ten thousand mile!

WILLIAM WORDSWORTH
(1770–1850)

'Surprised by joy –
impatient as the Wind'

Surprised by joy – impatient as the Wind
I turned to share the transport – Oh! with whom
But Thee, deep buried in the silent tomb,
That spot which no vicissitude can find?
Love, faithful love, recalled thee to my mind –
But how could I forget thee? Through what
      power,
Even for the least division of an hour,
Have I been so beguiled as to be blind
To my most grievous loss! – That thought's
      return
Was the worst pang that sorrow ever bore,
Save one, one only, when I stood forlorn,
Knowing my heart's best treasure was no more;
That neither present time, nor years unborn
Could to my sight that heavenly face restore.

Samuel Taylor Coleridge
(1772–1834)

To Lesbia

Vivamus, mea Lesbia, atque amemus.

Catullus

My Lesbia, let us love and live,
And to the winds, my Lesbia, give
Each cold restraint, each boding fear
Of age and all her saws severe.
Yon sun now posting to the main
Will set, – but 'tis to rise again; –
But we, when once our mortal light
Is set, must sleep in endless night.
Then come, with whom alone I'll live,
A thousand kisses take and give!
Another thousand! – to the store
Add hundreds – then a thousand more!
And when they to a million mount,
Let confusion take the account, –
That you, the number never knowing,
May continue still bestowing –
That I for joys may never pine,
Which never can again be mine!

LORD BYRON
(1788–1824)

from DON JUAN

They look'd up to the sky, whose floating glow
    Spread like a rosy ocean, vast and bright;
They gazed upon the glittering sea below,
    Whence the broad moon rose circling into sight;
They heard the wave's splash, and the wind so low,
    And saw each other's dark eyes darting light
Into each other – and, beholding this,
Their lips drew near, and clung into a kiss;

A long, long kiss, a kiss of youth, and love,
    And beauty, all concentrating like rays
Into one focus, kindled from above;
    Such kisses as belong to early days,
Where heart, and soul, and sense, in concert move,
    And the blood's lava, and the pulse a blaze,
Each kiss a heart-quake, – for a kiss's strength,
I think, it must be reckon'd by its length.

They were alone, but not alone as they
    Who shut in chambers think it loneliness;
The silent ocean, and the starlight bay,
    The twilight glow, which momently grew less,
The voiceless sands, and dropping caves, that lay
    Around them, made them to each other press,
As if there were no life beneath the sky
Save theirs, and that their life could never die.

They feared no eyes nor ears on that lone beach,
    They felt no terrors from the night; they were
All in all to each other; though their speech
    Was broken words, they *thought* a language
        there, –
And all the burning tongues the passions teach
    Found in one sigh the best interpreter
Of nature's oracle – first love, – that all
Which Eve has left her daughters since her fall.

Alas! they were so young, so beautiful,
    So lonely, loving, helpless, and the hour
Was that in which the heart is always full
    And, having o'er itself no further power,
Prompts deeds eternity can not annul,
    But pays off moments in an endless shower
Of hell-fire – all prepared for people giving
Pleasure or pain to one another living.

They look upon each other, and their eyes
    Gleam in the moonlight; and her white arm
        clasps
Round Juan's head, and his around her lies
    Half buried in the tresses which it grasps;
She sits upon his knee, and drinks his sighs,
    He hers, until they end in broken gasps;
And thus they form a group that's quite antique,
Half naked, loving, natural and Greek.

PERCY BYSSHE SHELLEY
(1792–1822)

from EPIPSYCHIDION

Spouse! Sister! Angel! Pilot of the Fate
Whose course has been so starless! O too late
Belovèd! O too soon adored, by me!
For in the fields of Immortality
My spirit should at first have worshipped thine,
A divine presence in a place divine;
Or should have moved beside it on this earth,
A shadow of that substance, from its birth;
But not as now: – I love thee; yes, I feel
That on the fountain of my heart a seal
Is set, to keep its waters pure and bright
For thee, since in those *tears* thou hast delight.
We – are we not formed, as notes of music are,
For one another, though dissimilar;
Such difference without discord, as can make
Those sweetest sounds, in which all spirits shake
As trembling leaves in a continuous air?

Thy wisdom speaks in me, and bids me dare
Beacon the rocks on which high hearts are wrecked.
I never was attached to that great sect,
Whose doctrine is, that each one should select
Out of the crowd a mistress or a friend,

And all the rest, though fair and wise, commend
To cold oblivion, though it is in the code
Of modern morals, and the beaten road
Which those poor slaves with weary footsteps tread,
Who travel to their home among the dead
By the broad highway of the world, and so
With one chained friend, perhaps a jealous foe,
The dreariest and the longest journey go.

True Love in this differs from gold and clay,
That to divide is not to take away.
Love is like understanding, that grows bright,
Gazing on many truths; 'tis like thy light,
Imagination! which from earth and sky,
And from the depths of human fantasy,
As from a thousand prisms and mirrors, fills
The Universe with glorious beams, and kills
Error, the worm, with many a sun-like arrow
Of its reverberated lightning. Narrow
The heart that loves, the brain that contemplates,
The life that wears, the spirit that creates
One object, and one form, and builds thereby
A sepulchre for its eternity.

JOHN KEATS
(1795–1821)

'When I have fears
that I may cease to be'

When I have fears that I may cease to be
    Before my pen has glean'd my teeming brain,
Before high-piled books, in charactery,
    Hold like rich garners the full ripen'd grain;
When I behold, upon the night's starr'd face,
    Huge cloudy symbols of a high romance,
And think that I may never live to trace
    Their shadows, with the magic hand of
        chance;
And when I feel, fair creature of an hour,
    That I shall never look upon thee more,
Never have relish in the faery power
    Of unreflecting love; – then on the shore
Of the wide world I stand alone, and think
Till love and fame to nothingness do sink.

ROBERT BROWNING
(1812–89)

'You'll love me yet! –
and I can tarry'

from PIPPA PASSES

You'll love me yet! – and I can tarry
    Your love's protracted growing:
June reared that bunch of flowers you carry,
    From seeds of April's sowing.

I plant a heartful now: some seed
    At least is sure to strike,
And yield – what you'll not pluck indeed,
    Not love, but, may be, like.

You'll look at least on love's remains,
    A grave's one violet:
Your look? – that pays a thousand pains.
    What's death? You'll love me yet!

ELIZABETH BARRETT BROWNING
(1806–61)

'How do I love thee?
Let me count the ways'

How do I love thee? Let me count the ways.
I love thee to the depth and breadth and height
My soul can reach, when feeling out of sight
For the ends of Being and ideal Grace.
I love thee to the level of everyday's
Most quiet need, by sun and candlelight.
I love thee freely, as men strive for Right;
I love thee purely, as they turn from Praise.
I love thee with the passion put to use
In my old griefs, and with my childhood's faith.
I love thee with a love I seemed to lose
With my lost saints, – I love thee with the
      breath,
Smiles, tears, of all my life! – and, if God
      choose,
I shall but love thee better after death.

EDGAR ALLAN POE
(1809–49)

To Helen

Helen, thy beauty is to me
    Like those Nicéan barks of yore,
That gently, o'er a perfumed sea,
    The weary, way-worn wanderer bore
    To his own native shore.

On desperate seas long wont to roam,
    Thy hyacinth hair, thy classic face,
Thy Naiad airs have brought me home
    To the glory that was Greece,
And the grandeur that was Rome.

Lo! in yon brilliant window-niche
    How statue-like I see thee stand,
    The agate lamp within thy hand!
Ah, Psyche, from the regions which
    Are Holy Land!

ALFRED LORD TENNYSON
(1809–92)

'Now sleeps the crimson petal, now the white'

'Now sleeps the crimson petal, now the
white;
Nor waves the cypress in the palace walk;
Nor winks the gold fin in the porphyry font:
The fire-fly wakens: waken thou with me.

Now droops the milkwhite peacock like a
ghost,
And like a ghost she glimmers on to me.

Now lies the Earth all Danaë to the stars,
And all thy heart lies open unto me.

Now slides the silent meteor on, and leaves
A shining furrow, as thy thoughts in me.

Now folds the lily all her sweetness up,
And slips into the bosom of the lake:
So fold thyself, my dearest, thou, and slip
Into my bosom and be lost in me.'

WALT WHITMAN
(1819–92)

'Once I pass'd through a populous city'

Once I pass'd through a populous city imprinting
    my brain for future use with its shows,
    architecture, customs, traditions,
Yet now of all that city I remember only a woman
    I casually met there who detain'd me for
    love of me,
Day by day and night by night we were together–
    all else has long been forgotten by me,
I remember I say only that woman who
    passionately clung to me,
Again we wander, we love, we separate again,
Again she holds me by the hand, I must not go,
I see her close beside me with silent lips sad and
    tremulous.

EMILY DICKINSON
(1830–86)

'If you were coming in the fall'

If you were coming in the fall,
I'd brush the summer by
With half a smile and half a spurn,
As housewives do a fly.

If I could see you in a year,
I'd wind the months in balls,
And put them each in separate drawers,
Until their time befalls.

If only centuries delayed,
I'd count them on my hand,
Subtracting till my fingers dropped
Into Van Diemen's land.

If certain, when this life was out,
That yours and mine, should be,
I'd toss it yonder, like a rind,
And taste eternity.

But now, uncertain of the length
Of time's uncertain wing,
It goads me, like the goblin bee,
That will not state its sting.

CHRISTINA ROSSETTI
(1830–94)

A Birthday

My heart is like a singing bird
    Whose nest is in a watered shoot;
My heart is like an apple-tree
    Whose boughs are bent with thickset
       fruit;
My heart is like a rainbow shell
    That paddles in a halcyon sea;
My heart is gladder than all these
    Because my love is come to me.

Raise me a dais of silk and down;
    Hang it with vair and purple dyes;
Carve it in doves and pomegranates,
    And peacocks with a hundred eyes;
Work it in gold and silver grapes,
    In leaves and silver fleurs-de-lys;
Because the birthday of my life
    Is come, my love is come to me.

THOMAS HARDY
(1840–1928)

The Voice

Woman much missed, how you call to me, call to
    me,
Saying that now you are not as you were
When you had changed from the one who was all
    to me,
But as at first, when our day was fair.

Can it be you that I hear? Let me view you, then,
Standing as when I drew near to the town
Where you would wait for me: yes, as I knew you
    then,
Even to the original air-blue gown!

Or is it only the breeze, in its listlessness
Travelling across the wet mead to me here,
You being ever dissolved to wan wistlessness,
Heard no more again far or near?

    Thus I; faltering forward,
    Leaves around me falling,
Wind oozing thin through the thorn from
    norward,
    And the woman calling.

WILLIAM BUTLER YEATS
(1865–1939)

Down by the Salley Gardens

Down by the salley gardens my love and I did
  meet;
She passed the salley gardens with little snow-
  white feet.
She bid me take love easy, as the leaves grow on
  the tree;
But I, being young and foolish, with her would not
  agree.

In a field by the river my love and I did stand,
And on my leaning shoulder she laid her snow-
  white hand.
She bid me take life easy, as the grass grows on the
  weirs;
But I was young and foolish, and now am full of
  tears.

ROBERT FROST
(1874–1963)

To Earthward

Love at the lips was touch
As sweet as I could bear;
And once that seemed too much;
I lived on air

That crossed me from sweet things
The flow of – was it musk
From hidden grapevine springs
Down hill at dusk?

I had the swirl and ache
From sprays of honeysuckle
That when they're gathered shake
Dew on the knuckle.

I craved strong sweets, but those
Seemed strong when I was young;
The petal of the rose
It was that stung.

Now no joy but lacks salt
That is not dashed with pain
And weariness and fault;
I crave the stain

Of tears, the aftermark
Of almost too much love,
The sweet of bitter bark
And burning clove.

When stiff and sore and scarred
I take away my hand
From leaning on it hard
In grass and sand,

The hurt is not enough:
I long for weight and strength
To feel the earth as rough
To all my length.

NOTES ON THE PICTURES

p.2   *Basket of Flowers* by Hans Looscher (1859–1923), Gavin Graham Gallery, London. Photo: Bridgeman Art Library, London.

p.8   *April,* from a book of hours by Simon Benninck, Victoria and Albert Museum, London. Crown copyright.

p.10   *Portrait of John Donne* (early seventeenth century), artist unknown. In the collection of the Marquis of Lothian.

p.13   *Venetia Stanley, Lady Digby* (c. 1615–17), miniature by Peter Oliver, reproduced by courtesy of the Board of Trustees of the Victoria and Albert Museum, London.

p.15   Frontispiece to *Songs of Experience* (1794), Library of Congress, Washington. Photo: Bridgeman Art Library, London.

p.35   *The Dawn of Love* (1846) by Thomas Brooks (1818–91), reproduced by courtesy of the Board of Trustees of the Victoria and Albert Museum, London.

p.19   *Morning amongst the Coniston Fells,* Cumberland (c. 1798) by J.M.W. Turner (1775–1851), Tate Gallery, London.

p.20   *A Scene in Leigh Woods* (detail) by Francis Danby (1793–1861), City of Bristol Museum and Art Gallery. Photo: Bridgeman Art Library, London.

p.23   *Haidée, A Greek Girl* by Sir Charles Lock Eastlake (1793–1865), reproduced by courtesy of the Trustees of the Tate Gallery, London.

p.25   *Don Juan Discovered by Haidée* by Ford Madox Brown (1821–93), Musée d'Orsay, Paris. Photo: Lauros Giraudon/ Bridgeman Art Library, London.

p.27   *The Birth of Venus* (detail) by Sandro Botticelli (1444–1510), Uffizi Gallery, Florence.

p.29   *Madonna Lilies in a Garden* (1908) by Walter Crane (1845–1915), private collection. Photo: Bridgeman Art Library, London.

p.30   *John Keats* by Joseph Severn (1793–1879), National Portrait Gallery, London.

p.32   *Italian Landscape* (detail) by Samuel Palmer (1805–81), reproduced by courtesy of the Board of Trustees of the Victoria and Albert Museum, London. Photo: Bridgeman Art Library, London.

p.34   *Robert Browning* (1855) by Dante Gabriel Rossetti (1828–82), reproduced by permission of the Syndics of the Fitzwilliam Museum, Cambridge.

p.37   'To Helen', illustration by Edmund Dulac (1882–1953) from *The Bells and Other Poems* (1912) by Edgar Allan Poe, reproduced by permission of Hodder and Stoughton Ltd.

p.39   *Landscape at Night* (detail) by Nathan Theodore Fielding (*op.* 1775–1818), University of Liverpool Art Gallery and Collections. Photo: Bridgeman Art Library, London.

p.41   *Portrait of Maud Cook* (1895) by Thomas Eakins (1844–1916), reproduced by courtesy of Yale University Art Gallery, Connecticut. Bequest of Stephen Carlton Clarke, 1903.

p.43   *Storm Clouds, Maine* (1906–7) by Marsden Hartley (1877–1943), Walker Art Center, Minneapolis. Gift of the T.B. Walker Foundation.

p.45   *Reverie* (1868) by Dante Gabriel Rossetti (1828–82), reproduced by courtesy of Christie's, London. Photo: Bridgeman Art Library, London.

p.46   *Sterne's Maria* by William Powell Frith (1819–1909), private collection. Photo: Bridgeman Art Library, London.

p. 48 *The Garden of Eden* (1900) by Hugh Goldwyn Riviere (1869–1956), reproduced by courtesy of Guildhall Art Gallery, London. Photo: Bridgeman Art Library, London.

p.51 *In the Orchard* (1881) by Sir George Clausen (1852–1944), Salford Museums and Art Galleries. Photo: Bridgeman Art Library, London.

p.53 *Disappointed Love* (exhibited 1821) by Francis Danby (1793–1861), reproduced by courtesy of the Board of Trustees of the Victoria and Albert Museum, London.

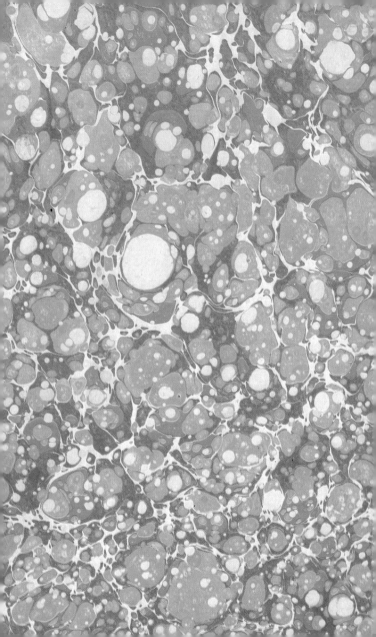